Look Twice!

Use the mirror to find
pairs of opposites

ABOVE

LEFT

RIGHT

Duncan Birmingham

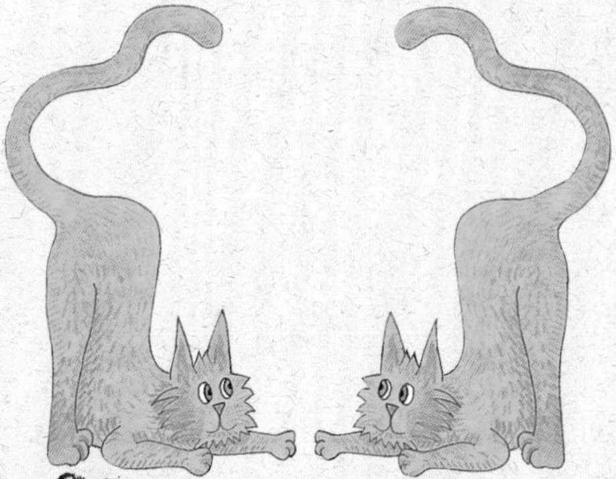

BELOW

TARQUIN PUBLICATIONS

Word pairs - Mirror pairs

There is a powerful connection between the ideas of pairs of words with opposite meanings and the properties of mirror images. Just as "left" and "right" can be regarded as opposites or duals, so reflection in a mirror reverses left and right. All the pictures in this book and their associated word pairs explore the notion of duality. For instance, one of the pictures shows a man who is either strong or weak according to the way that the mirror is facing. Another shows a cupboard which is either full or empty. Both images use the same reflection line, but with the mirror facing either left or right. Looking twice in the mirror at the same picture emphasises the duality of opposites. The idea of a room being tidy requires the dual idea that a room could be untidy. Of course in ordinary life there are all possible degrees of untidiness between tidy and untidy, just as there are shades of grey between black and white. However in this book we confine the shades of grey to the background colour of the pages and the pictures and the word pairs deal only with simple opposites!

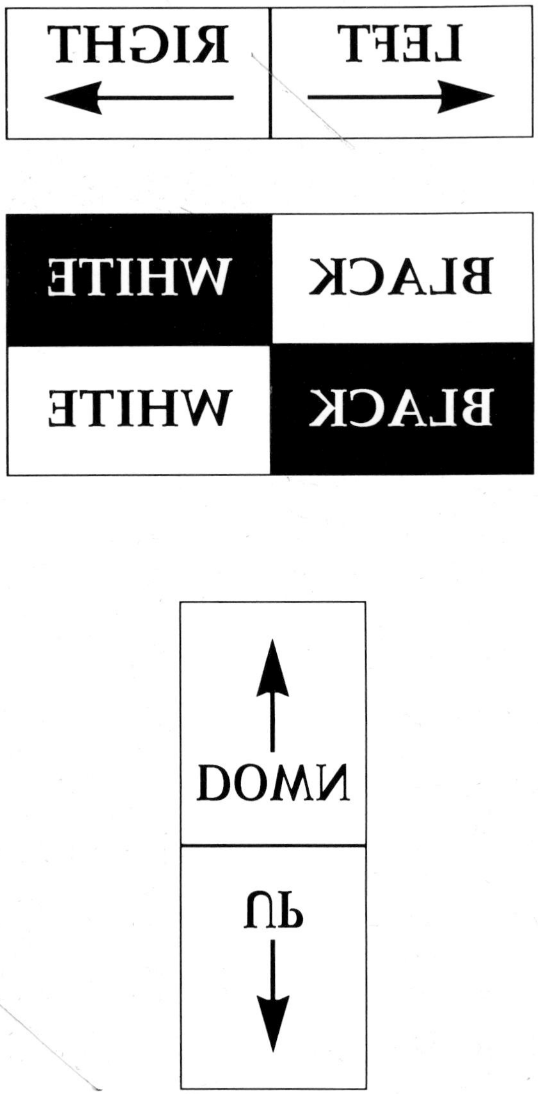

The primary aim of this book is for it to be amusing and fun, and that its more serious educational function should remain well hidden. On most occasions the searches for the pictures to match the words and the use of a mirror to read mirror writing are sufficiently interesting and absorbing that nothing more is called for. However most people at some time do become fascinated by the idea of opposites and mystified by the properties of mirror symmetry and want to know more. On such occasions, the reader, parents or teachers may find it useful to have some suggestions for experiments and investigations which can be used or not as the need arises. A selection of such ideas is given inside the back cover.

Look Twice!

O*** or C***** ?

OPEN OR CLOSED?

H**** or L**** ?

HEAVY OR LIGHT?

USE THE MIRROR TO FIND PAIRS OF OPPOSITES!

Look Twice!

**** or **** ?

*** or ** ?

YOU OR ME?

HOME OR AWAY?

****** or ******** ?

******** or ********* ?

FLYING OR PERCHING?

STARTING OR FINISHING?

***** or *** ?

*** or **** ?

NIGHT OR DAY?

FAT OR THIN?

Which is up and witches down?

Serious play or gone away?

**** or ***** ?

***** or ***** ?

**** or **** ?

TIGHT OR LOOSE?

PULL OR PUSH?

LONG OR SHORT?

Look Twice!

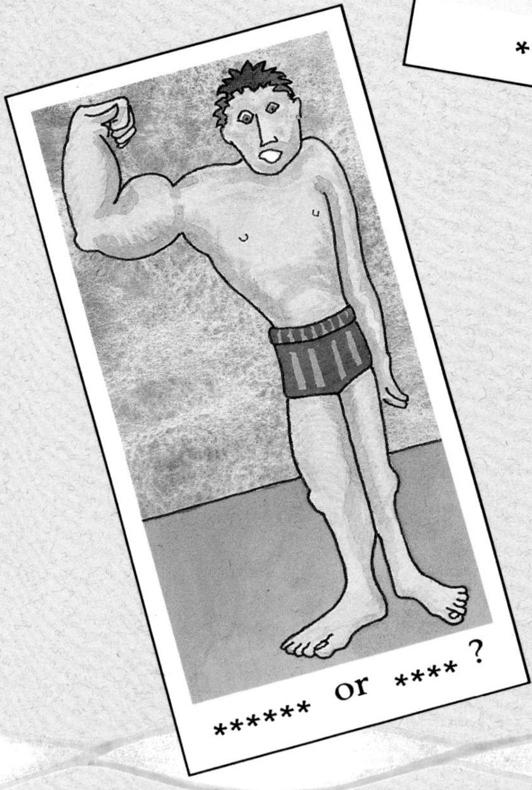

APPLES AND PEARS?

STRONG OR WEAK?

**** or **** ?

****** or ***** ?

SOFT OR FIRM?

ASLEEP OR AWAKE?

***** or **** ?

***** or **** ?

ALIVE OR DEAD?

LIGHT OR DARK?

The Haves or Have-Nots?

A prince who is sleeping or a prince who is peeping?

*** or **** ?

***** or ******* ?

*** or *** ?

SHOUT OR WHISPER?

RED OR BLUE?

WET OR DRY?

Look Twice!

I******ED or U*********ED ?

G*****ED or S******ED ?

GATHERED OR SCATTERED?

INHABITED OR UNINHABITED?

S*********ED or C****ED ?

J****ED or D****ED ?

STRAIGHTENED OR CRIMPED?

JUGGLED OR DROPPED?

****** or ***** ?

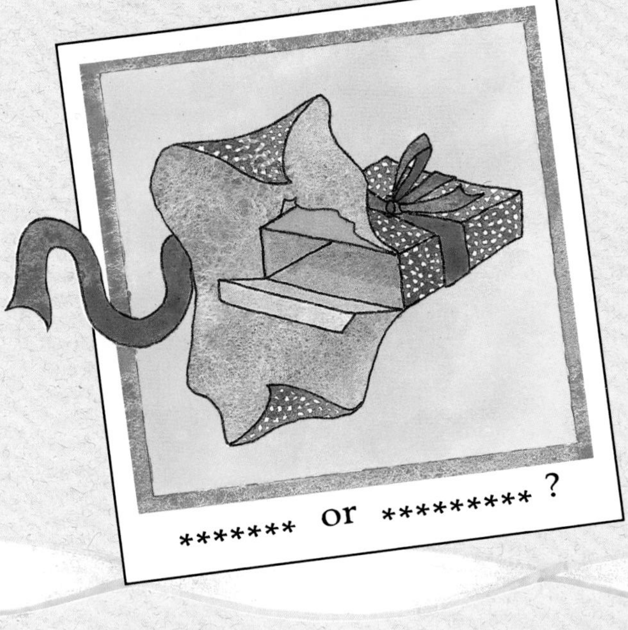

******* or ********* ?

WRAPPED OR UNWRAPPED?

BEFORE OR AFTER?

****** or *** ?

ANCIENT OR MODERN?

FRIEND OR FOE?

******* or ****** ?

******** or ****** ?

***** or ***** ?

ORDER OR CHAOS?

STARTLED OR SERENE?

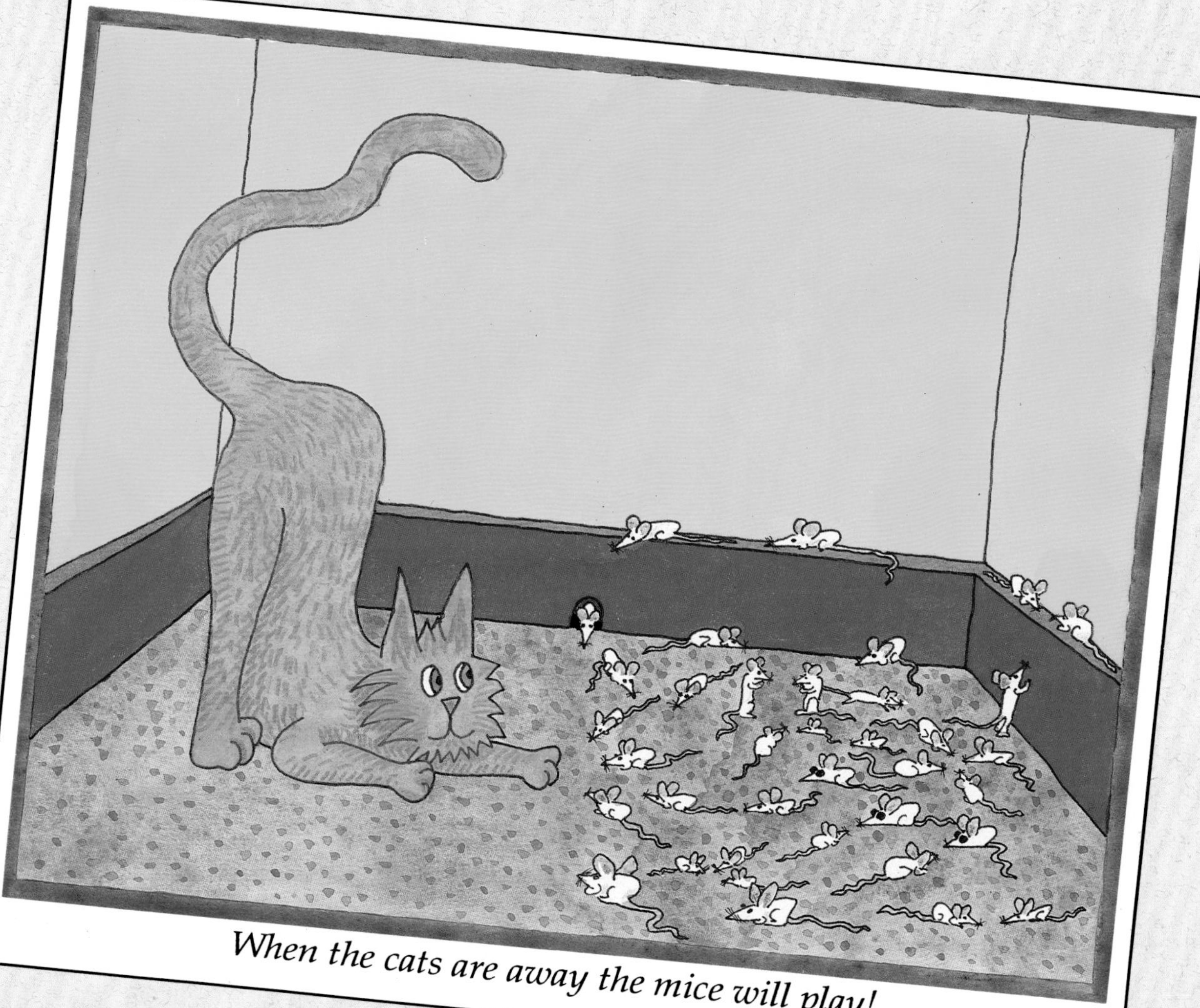

When the cats are away the mice will play!

Are they coming or going?

******* or ******* ?

***** or ****** ?

RESTING OR PLAYING?

LIONS OR TIGERS?

***** or ****** ?

**** or ****** ?

HOUSE OR GARDEN?

TIDY OR UNTIDY?

HAPPY OR SAD?

CAGED OR FREE?

CHILD OR GROWN-UP?

***** or *** ?

***** or **** ?

***** or ***** ** ?

**** or ****** ?

******** or ***** ?

TOGETHER OR APART?

HILL OR VALLEY?

Which is heavier a pound of feathers or a pound of lead?

Tree-man or he-man?

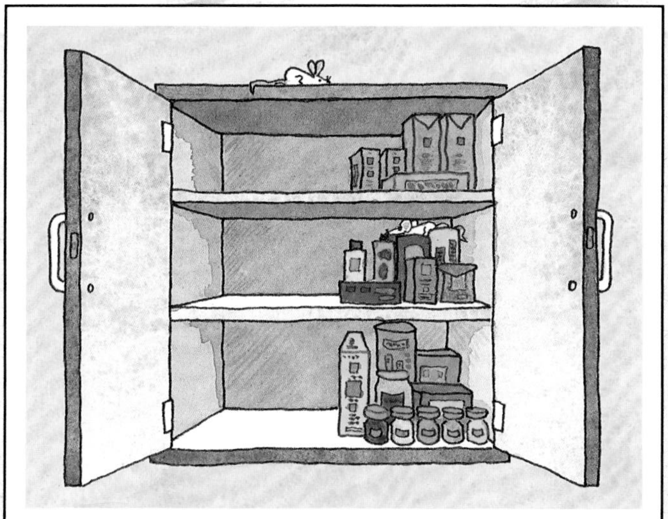

***** or **** ?

OUTSIDE OR INSIDE?

DIRTY OR CLEAN?

EMPTY OR FULL?

***** or ***** ?

******* or ****** ?

Look Twice!

C**** or T***** ?

L*** or I***** ?

A CREST is when
the boat is higher than the water.
A TROUGH is when
the water is higher than the boat.

A LAKE is
water surrounded by land.
An ISLAND is
land surrounded by water.

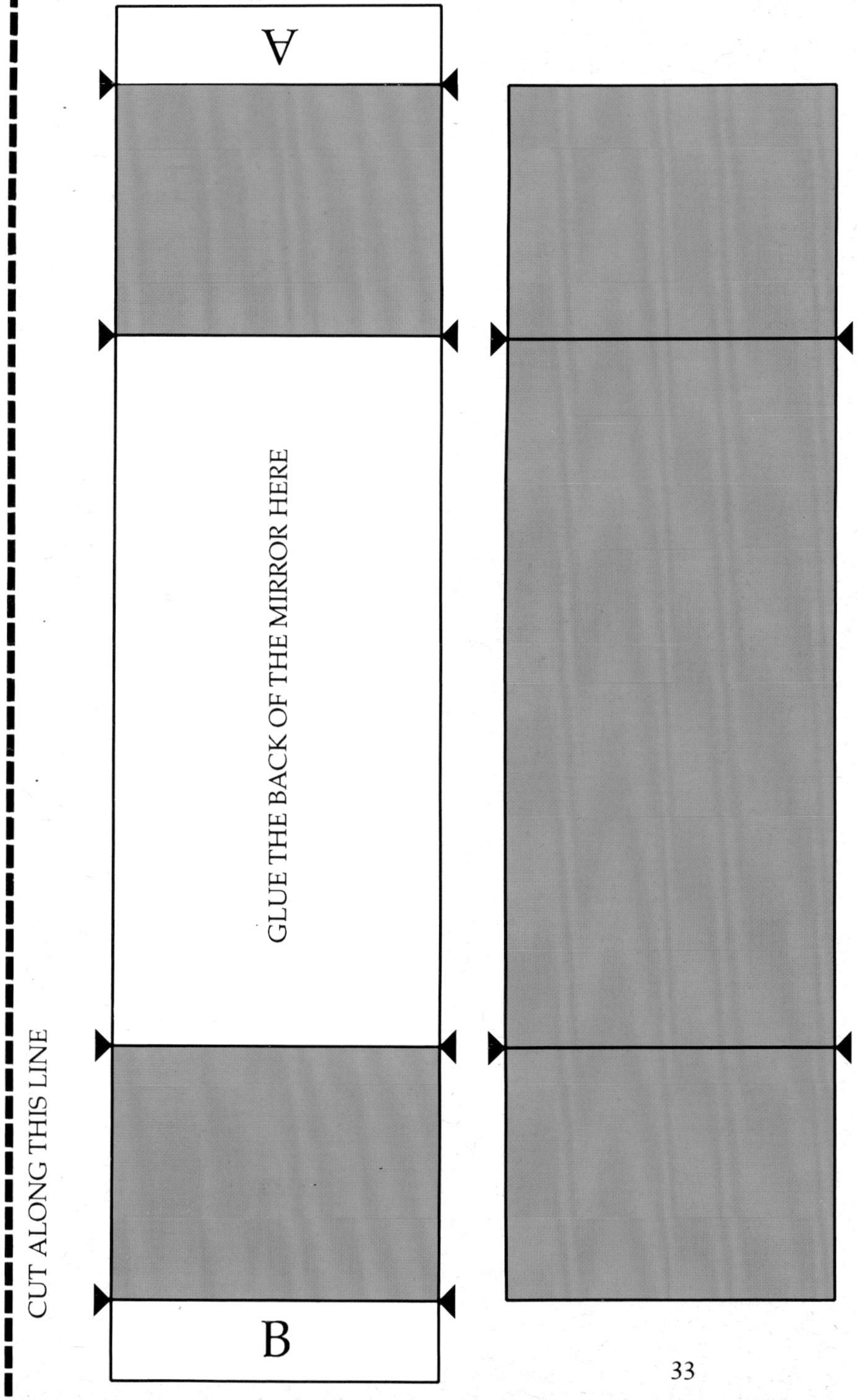

THE MIRROR STAND

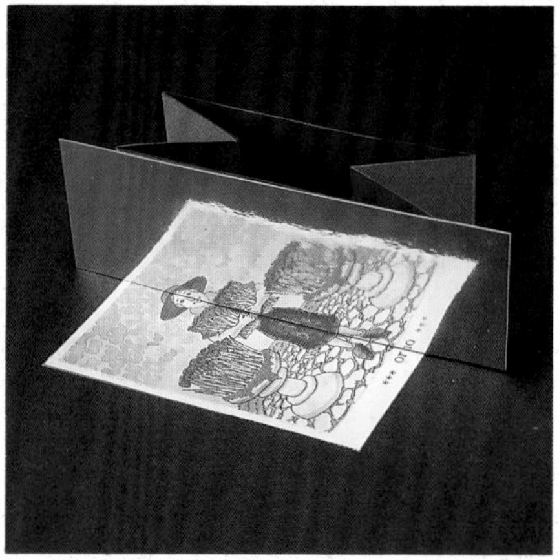

HOW TO MAKE THE STAND

1. Remove this page from the book.

2. Score along all lines marked.

3. Cut out precisely.

4. Crease along all fold lines and then glue the stand together using flaps A and B.

5. Glue the back of the mirror to the stand.

A

B